What the critics have said ab

★ ★ ★ ★

His mind is amazing. The audience was swept into his world—a world of lies, illusions, love and self-discovery. . . . Not to be missed.
—*Adelaide Advertiser*

Rapid-fire and hilarious.
—*Globe and Mail*

A smart, funny, highly entertaining look at one of Canada's least-known areas . . . a cool, mile-a-minute performance that's so thick with truisms, Canadianisms and various other isms, you could cross from Labrador to Newfoundland on the backs of them—just like the legendary codfish of old.
—*Vancouver Courier*

★ ★ ★ ★ ★

In an overstuffed Fringe world where quick, simple labels are often applied, the talents of TJ Dawe cannot be quantified.
—*Edmonton Sun*

The must-see show of this year's Fringe Festival . . . rich and layered.
—*Eye Weekly*

TJ Dawe is so consistently original that he has become one of my favourite Fringe performers . . . he made me weep. What makes *Labrador* really clever, though, is that Dawe turns this emotion on its head, revealing the lovely mechanics of theatre itself.
—*Georgia Straight*

TJ Dawe's *Labrador* is one of the most brilliant comic monologues ever delivered at two in the morning.

—*Montreal Gazette*

If you let yourself, you'll be drawn in by his disarming tale of discovering danger and beauty.

—*Orlando Sentinel*

Labrador is definitely a trip worth taking.

—*Orlando Weekly*

★ ★ ★ ★ ★

One of the must-sees of the year.

—*Saskatoon Star-Phoenix*

★ ★ ★ ★

Dawe has a quicksilver mind and an Uzi-burst style of delivery that will make you find it hard to enjoy more conventional one-man shows . . . dazzlingly funny.

—*Toronto Star*

All Dawe's considerable talents . . . are on display in this quirky new one-man show about his adventures, both real and imagined, as part of a touring children's show in a part of Canada about which very few of us know anything beyond where it hangs on the map. Funny, endearing stuff.

—*Toronto Sun*

Dawe has storytelling down to a fine art . . . this man's timing and delivery, and the accuracy of his eye on Canada's extremities, are masterful.

—*Vancouver Sun*

It's funny, affecting stuff. There are some poignant moments, and you sense Dawe has more to say without losing his edge and sense of humour . . . Underlines just how vapid and limp so many stand-up and/or comic one person acts are these days.

—*Edmonton Journal*

Dawe's determinedly lopsided view of the world—a blend of Jerry Seinfeld's observational humour and writer Sherwood Anderson's love of the peculiar—makes the mundane intriguing.

—*Victoria Times Colonist*

After witnessing *Labrador* firsthand, it's not hard to figure out what all the excitement is about . . . There is a depth to his wise-cracking that is intoxicating.

—*Winnipeg Free Press*

Labrador is not a show about a dog.

—*Adelaide Sunday Mail*

Labrador

Labrador
a one-person show
TJ Dawe

BRINDLE
& GLASS

© T.J. Dawe 2003

For more info on TJ Dawe or information on stage production rights visit www.tjdawe.com and www.pkfproductions.com

National Library of Canada Cataloguing in Publication
Dawe, T. J. (Ti-Jon David), 1974–
Labrador / TJ Dawe.

A play.
ISBN 0-9732481-2-2

I. Title.

PS8557.A84697L32 2003   C812'.6   C2003-906139-6

Cover and author photos: Michael Rinald

Author's acknowledgements: John Verhaeven, Linda Delcourt, my parents, all of my relatives in Newfoundland, Jeremy Hechtman, Patrick Goddard, Rachael Wilson, Michael Rinaldi, Mike Low, Bartocz Barczak, Janet Michael and David Ross at Western Canada Theatre, Duncan Low at the Cultch, Kelly Finnegan at PKF productions, Janet Munsil at Intrepid Theatre, Janet Coutts, Andrew Clark, Andrew Litzky and Llysa Holland. And everyone who ran and volunteered at the many fringe festivals where *Labrador* played. Also thanks to Jim Leard at Story Theatre Victoria, Jennifer Shore, and Robert, Ken and Alison from that tour. Very special thanks to Ruth Linka and Lee Shedden.

Brindle & Glass Publishing
www.brindleandglass.com

Brindle & Glass is committed to protecting the environment and to the responsible use of natural resources. This book is printed on 100% post-consumer recycled and ancient forest-friendly paper. For more information please visit www.oldgrowthfree.com.

1 2 3 4 5 06 05 04 03

PRINTED AND BOUND IN CANADA

Dedicated to my father and my grandfather.

Production Credits

Labrador was first performed as part of Two Night Stand
May 28 and 29, 1999
at the Cavern, Vancouver

Produced by Construction Ink, helmed by John Verhaeven
Stage Managed by Linda Delcourt
Lights and Sound run by John Verhaeven

Music before and after all performances was from North Atlantic
Dance by Newfoundland guitarist Gordon Quinton, a man with the
nimble fingers of the gods.

Notes on Irregular Grammar and Punctuation

Not all lines begin with a capital letter. Nor do they all end with a
punctuation mark. Nor do they all reach the end of the page. Some
words in the middle of sentences begin with capital letters for no reason any English teacher would ever approve of. Many sentences are
mere fragments. The Microsoft Word version of this script is riddled
with angry green underlinings. And quite a few red ones. All of this
is done to simulate the performance of the show, the delivery of the
lines. These transgressions are deliberate.

Labrador

(A chair, centre stage. A small paper lunch bag on it. Six couch cushions next to it, stage right.

A spotlight comes up, stage left of the chair.
A masking tape X marks the spot at the centre of it.

An actor walks on stage, places his feet on either side of the X, and speaks.)

People always lie at funerals

They give speeches about the dead person, but they only say the
   good things

He Was Kind
He Had Courage
He Was an Inspiration to Everyone Who Knew Him

BULLSHIT

Who was this guy, St Francis of Assisi??

If a race of aliens from outer space were to study us from our eulo-
   gies, and nothing else, they'd come up with the conclusion that
   every single human being on this planet was *Unbelievably*
   Fantastic!!

so what if people said the bad things

He was Cheap
He never gave you a ride home, even if you really needed one, and
    he knew you needed one, and he had nothing better to do any-
    way, and it was raining
and
He was a Boring Conversationalist

I hope they tell the truth at my funeral

I'm not dead

Obviously

But I will be—someday, somehow
And when I go, I hope at least one person is honest and stands up
    and says

He was up and down
He'd get depressed sometimes for no reason
He'd remember the oddest things
And he was never really that sure of what was going on

(Actor reaches over, takes the bag, reaches into it and pulls out a . . .)

Anybody want a banana?
Anyone?

Anyone hungry?

(Ad lib as necessary until someone from the audience agrees to eat the banana. Actor goes and gives it to them.)

Thanks
I'm going to need the peel in about twenty minutes, so put it in
    this bag
But you've got lots of time

(Actor returns to the spotlight, and carefully places his feet on either side of the X again.)

Okay

Let us Begin

(With a broad gesture:)

Labrador!

What does anyone know about . . .

Labrador!

What does everyone know about Labrador

Well . . .

It's to the north, and to the east of practically everywhere
It's physically attached to Quebec
And it's politically and culturally attached to Newfoundland

Newfoundland—that's what anyone knows about Labrador
Newfoundland and Labrador go together by mental association,
    they're practically one word: Newfoundland-n-Labrador
Just like Salt & Pepper
Laurel & Hardy
Batman & Robin
Alsace & Lorraine
Newfoundland & Labrador

And that's about it
Really?
Yep
That's all anyone knows
What's the capital city
Is there a capital city
Or is St. John's the capital of Newfoundland and Labrador
What are the major cities
Are there any major cities
Are there any cities period
What language is spoken there predominantly, is it English or
    French
Or whatever language it is, is it spoken with a Quebec accent or a
    Newfoundland accent
What would French spoken with a Newfoundland accent conceiv-
    ably sound like

Has anyone famous ever come from there
Has anything famous historically ever happened there
What's the industry
What are the exports
What are the imports
Why would anyone move there
Why would anyone live there
Does anyone live there
What the Hell's it Like?

don't know

And that's okay—that is okay

There's a lot of things like that—little, simple, everyday things that
    most people, including me, don't know

Why is the sky blue

I don't know!
I mean, I'm sure someone knows, I'm sure it's not secret informa-
    tion, I'm sure it's been researched and documented and written
    in a book but I've never read that book

Who is the Head of State of Denmark
What's their title. Is it the premier? The prime minister? The presi-
    dent? The chancellor? The King?
The Great Dane?

How do mirrors work? You know? I mean, I know it's reflective
  glass and everything, but . . . how does it do that? The glass in
  a window doesn't do that—not quite
What's on the other side of the mirror that makes the one side
  reflect perfectly but the other side not be involved at all—not
  even exist

Or, if you shine a light in a mirror, does it make the room twice as
  bright?

How do they get the ratings for radio stations
No one has ever asked me who I listen to
Do they have a machine that knows who's tuning in to what?

Why do you get the hiccups? It's not from eating too fast, that's an
  old wives' tale
I eat fast all the time and don't get them—when I get the hiccups,
  they'll just happen—what is that?

If dogs really do have such an acute sense of smell, then how is it
  that they can stick their nose right up another dog's ass and
  sniff sniff sniff away?

Bread
Who invented bread?
How did they think of that?
Milling wheat into flour—that's a very strange first step, especially
  if no one's ever done it before—and then taking this magical
  new substance and mixing it with perfect proportions of water

and milk and butter and eggs and sugar and salt and yeast
and mixing it into dough and then kneading the dough and kneading and kneading and kneading and kneading . . .

Kneading

The word 'Kneading' begins with a K

A Silent K

Why

Why have a K if it's gonna be silent?

Why have silent letters period?—the K in Kneading, the P in
Pneumonia, the G in Gnat, the W in answer—what's the
matter with this language

It's like how some people, out there, instead of saying "Schedule"
will actually say "Shhhhedule"

It's a Schedule, dammit!

A schedule's a very rigid and disciplined thing, it needs the hard,
percussive K, otherwise it's all flabby and impotent, it's a
"shhhhedule"

But getting back to bread—the milling the mixing the kneading
the kneading the kneading

And then baking at a very specific temperature for a very specific
amount of time until it rises and turns golden brown, which it
certainly didn't do the first time someone tried to bake a loaf

What an obscure process—how'd they come up with this in all
these different primitive cultures all over the world

Or there's the elevator question—you know? The Elevator
Question

Let's say you're riding in a normal elevator, minding your own business and then . . .

cable snaps, you're plummeting down the shaft, you're going to die, oh no.

Now—if you time it just right and jump at the last second—will that save your life?

Will that make any difference at all—because if you're falling you're going down, but if you're jumping you're going up—or are you? Are you still falling, just not quite as fast? Is the fact that your feet aren't connected to the floor at the moment of impact—does that neutralize the physics of the equation—I don't know

Or, in a movie—what exactly does the Executive Producer do

What do any of those people in the credits do—aside from the obvious ones—why do they show us those hundreds of names? Do they really think anyone out here cares about who the Gaffer is? And the Key Grip and the Dolly Grip and Caterers and the Stunt Men and the Stand-Ins and the Unit Line Production Manager?

What if everything was like that? What if everything in the world came with credits

Shirts—You buy a shirt and there's this long list attached to it of all the names of the people who grew the cotton and picked it and sewed it in the sweatshop and folded it, trucked it, shipped it, put on the shelf and sold it to you, right down to the name of the guy who drew the little circles on the tag that show you how to wash the thing so it doesn't shrink

Or acknowledgments in a book

Before the book starts there's a page of acknowledgments

Special Thanks To, it says, and then a list of all these names
Who are these people?
No one I know—no one anyone knows!
The only person who knows who these people are is . . . the
  Author!
Then thank 'em in person, send them flowers
Do you really think anyone in the reading public is going to stop
  before they read your book and moon over all these names and
  say "I'll bet those people are all just . . . swell"

Or TV credits—at the end of a TV show they screel the names past
  you so fast you can't possibly read them
Then why fucking show them?
It's like they're barely complying with a rule they hate—then why's
  it a rule?

Or laugh track! That's the craziest one of all
Why do we have laugh tracks on our sitcoms
That is absolutely going to baffle archaeologists two thousand years
  from now
They're going to discover this and present it at a conference and say
"Look at this: the television itself seems to be laughing at the jokes"

All of these things—these mysteries of everyday life—there's a mil-
  lion of 'em
It makes me so glad I don't have a kid because a kid would be asking about them
and more—weird ones I could never think of in advance
and asking with these great big expectant moon eyes

to me, the omniscient adult
but I wouldn't know
so I'd either have to say that or make something up
and that's the choice between letting the world come crashing
    down on this bright, innocent little bundle of humanity now

or letting it come crashing down later

and what kind of a choice

is that

so

I went

To

Labrador

And I thought—at least I'll know about that one

So I did

I got on a plane and flew from one side of this country to the other
Off to that obscure corner of Canada

In the winter

And I found out who I am

And I fell in love

With the most beautiful woman in the world

And I got the shit beat out of me

With a shovel

But that comes later
First—the Exposition, the Explanation
Because it's not like I was just sitting in a chair and thought
    "Labrador . . ." and then went there

Not at all
Not even close

There was a whole web of circumstances

I just hesitate to get into it because it leads me into what I consider
    to be
Ugly Territory

But it's unavoidable, so Fuck It, here we go

Domino Number One in the sequence of events that sent me to
    Labrador
Domino Number One . . .

I Am An Actor

Okay, there we go, I've said it and it's done
And that's Domino Number One, that's it
And I hate saying it, especially in a show
And it's not false modesty, it's just this huge peeve of mine because

A) I'm standing here doing a one-person show right now
Therefore, it's obvious that I'm an actor
Doesn't need to be said
A bus driver doesn't turn around while they're driving and harass
    the passengers saying
"Hey, I'm a bus driver, I'm driving this bus you know, I'm driving
    this bus because I'm a Bus Driver, I'm Bus Driver, I'm a Bus
    Driver"

It's obvious

B) I can't stand it when actors come up to you and tell you they're
    an actor
If you ask, that's fine
If it comes up in the course of natural conversation, that's fine too
But normally it's not like that
No one asks
No one cares!

But an actor will walk right up to you and lay the sauce on for you
And then voila, there's no ignoring it
Everything about them screams that they are, or would like to be,
   an actor
Everything:
The voice
The voices
The volume they speak at so they can play the whole room while
   pretending they're just having a conversation with you
The grandiose gestures they'll employ so everyone can see them as
   well as hear them
The kooky character voices
And nutty foreign accents they'll slip into for NO REASON AT ALL
The pregnant pauses before the

(pause)

punchlines
The fact that there even are punchlines
The way they twist natural conversation into a series of set-ups and
   pauses and punchlines
so that they can make it seem like with them the entertainment
   just never stops, life is a roving cabaret of non-stop amuse-
   ment—when in fact these are prepared conversational routines
   that they've foisted on dozens of other people—people who
   didn't want to hear them either—who wished that they would
   just shut the fuck up and save it for the stage!

I can't stand that

Why would you be like that?

And

C)

I

Hate

Actors

Writing

And

Performing

One

Person

Shows

About

Them

Being An Actor!!

Because WHY are we, the audience, supposed to care about how
   your career is going? Your ACTING career?
What is the gist of that? What would triumph in a show like that
   be? I guess that would be . . . Getting the Big Part, and all the
   Big Parts that follow that—Fame, Fortune, Stardom, Success,
   Being Whisked Up and Off, Above and Away from the Little
   People, the Plebes—Us—the Audience
Oh—that's a beautiful sentiment to have—especially at the middle
   of a show
That's like rock stars who write songs—who write albums—who
   write rock operas about how much it sucks to be a rock star
Hmm. Yeah. I'm with ya. Must be tough
Or stand-up comedians that do their entire routine without ever
   once straying from the topic that they are a stand-up comedian
Isn't the idea to talk about something else?
Or novelists who write a novel about a novelist who's having trou-
   ble writing a novel
Or screenplays! Screenplays . . . not just screenplays about people
   writing screenplays, but screenplays in general—and not so
   much the screenplays themselves as the people writing them—
   and not so much people writing screenplays as people "work-
   ing on" screenplays
Working on a Screenplay
People like to lay that one on you like it means something
"Oh yeah—I'm . . . Working on a Screenplay"
What does that mean? Someone commissioned you to write a
   screenplay?
"Well . . . no. I'm just working on it. On my own"
Oh—so it's just something you're doing. Well I'm reading a book!

I'm going to the supermarket to buy some purple onions
I mean as long as we're just listing the things we're doing, why stop
there? Why not go right down to breathing!

All of this—actors getting off on being actors and writers getting
off on being writers and comedians getting off on being comedians it all just makes me retch

And that's what I'm doing right now
Not retching—but a one-person show
About an actor
Where the person just stands up there and talks about themselves
And the script ends with the beginning

But it's part of the story, it's not the whole story, it's only Domino
Number One

And it's done

Kind of bleeds over into Domino Number Two, but we're almost
done with it, I promise

Domino Number Two
As an actor, I got a Job
An Acting Job
A Tour

Tour—that's a word I love
The rock bands have done a lot of work to glamourize the word

"tour" since about 1964

"Tour"—instantly, by mental association, means a World Tour—a
World Tour in Stadiums—in Sold Out Stadiums—in Sold Out
Stadiums full of Roadies and Groupies and Screaming Fans!

No

Children's theatre

Small towns, school gyms
Two shows a day, sometimes three
Different school, sometimes different town every show
Five days a week
Nine months a year—September to June, as long as there's kids in
schools to play to
Living in a van
Eating in cafés
Sleeping in motels
About 250 performances before the contract is up
Blue-Collar Theatre

But it's a job
And it's a job acting
And it's a tour
And even though "tour" doesn't mean some of those other things,
it does mean travel, and I love travelling, even to bad places,
just makes life stretch like saltwater taffy
And, by a particular stroke of luck, this particular tour, after a cer-
tain number of months, will take you to . . .

Newfoundland

Well now

That rang something special for me
You see, my dad's from St. John's
His whole side of the family's there—he's the only one who left
Pardon me—he's the only one who left and didn't go back
They all go back
Not just his family, but anyone from that province
I don't know why—doesn't seem like an easy place to live
But if you grew up there, there's a magic about the place that gets
    into your blood and bones and nothing can keep you away—
    nothing
Not the insane weather that sometimes brings ice and snow in
    June—I'd hear this on the phone from my grandparents
Not the complete economic collapse that killed the fishing industry
    and has made it absolutely impossible to find a job of any
    kind, for anyone
Not the twelve per cent provincial sales tax, plus GST
Nothing can stop the wandering Newfoundlander from wanting,
    needing, having to come
Home
That's what they call it: Home
They never say Newfoundland
And the way a Newfoundlander says it, the word has its full value,
    that extra oomph, that tinge in the voice
Home
The place you do nothing but miss when you're away

And that brings you comfort and solace and joy when you return

Except for my dad
He left when he was seventeen
Went to New York, went to University there
Became a teacher, later a principal
Got his first teaching job in Victoria
Then moved to Vancouver
Met my mom in Seattle—she's from Iowa
They got married in Toronto
Moved back to Vancouver
Then Whitehorse
Then Vancouver
I was born there
I grew up there
They still live there

And all those years and all those cities my dad lost his
    Newfoundland accent
Didn't play the fiddle, couldn't fish
Never told stories about the Old Days, the Hard Times
It's as if he was born at thirty
Growing up his family hadn't had a camera, so I had no idea what
    he looked like as a kid, teenager, young man, what his house
    looked like, friends looked like, nothing—I had no image of
    Newfoundland
Other than that garnered from Newfie jokes
Or *The Shipping News*
Or this one photo my grandmother sent one Christmas, mid-eighties

I don't know why it stuck with me, but it did

It was her at her sister's place in Twillingate

Twillingate's a squid town in the north of the island part of
    Newfoundland

The industry there—when there was one—was squid

They'd jig—fish—for squid about the size and shape of a dish-
    washing glove

They catch them by the net-load, and then pin them up with
    clothespins on the clotheslines in the back of all the houses

They'd leave them there for several days until they dried, then
    they'd take them down, pack them up in crates, ship them off

They'd eventually be unpacked, chopped, breaded and deep-fried

Calamari

So that's my image of Newfoundland: Squid on the clothesline

And now, some years later, I'm being flown there for free

PAID!

Paid to tour the Land of my Ancestors

That's like getting a Guggenheim grant

And and and and and . . . not just Newfoundland . . .

Labrador

Labrador, where my grandfather's originally from—left as a very
    small child, doesn't remember it

But that's where his background's from

Where his ancestors—therefore *my* ancestors—came to from the
    Old Country, whatever old country that was, I'm not sure

But that is where my last name is supposedly as common as Smith

Think of that

Maybe I'll go there and everyone'll look

Kind of like

Me

(Actor checks to see that he's still in position, adjusts if necessary.)

Okay—now at this point in the show, if I were a smoker, I'd pull
    out a cigarette, light it, and smoke it, but mostly hold it and
    continue talking

And everyone would see this

The smokers would see it and think "Hey, I could go for a smoke"
And the non-smokers would see it and think "He's smoking"

And when people's attention wandered from the story, or from
    the one voice going on and on and on and on and on and
    on and on
As it does for the whole show, rest assured
They could take a break
And watch the pluming smoke
Rise into the light

But I don't smoke

Tobacco

So, cut to seven months later in the timeline
Tour started early September, it's based in Victoria, it's now
    early March
And for these first seven months we've toured BC exclusively
Up, down, sideways, diagonal, all over the place, there's no logic to
    the way this tour was booked, it's the Star of David tour

We've done about 180 shows at this point
Average 350 kids a school
And in our show we meet them at the gym doors and seat them
    class by class in semi-circles on the gym floor

So that's face-to-face contact with about thirty thousand kids
Now I haven't been around that many kids since I *was* one
And there's this crazy thing
I never noticed

If you look at the face of a child in just the right way
And anyone can do this, it's totally easy—
You can see their parents
Even if you've never met their parents
Especially if you've never met their parents
You can see that this is a young, untouched version of an older face

Stops you in your tracks

Makes you think about those parents
How they were once that age
And that size
And that innocent
And they looked just like that

But then time passed
They grew
And they copied themselves

And these little copies'll grow and copy themselves
And their little copies'll grow and copy themselves
And their little copies'll grow and copy themselves
For a thousand generations to come
Like it's always been, going back a thousand generations

Wild.

But

Thirty thousand kids later

The novelty of this

Has long worn off

180 consecutive shows

I can't think of anything I've done 180 times consecutively, much
    less

the Same

Show

It has become like Factory Work

Well, not quite

I have done factory work

The summer I turned sixteen, I worked on the assembly line at a
    packaging plant
Screwing caps on bottles, putting bottles in boxes
Screwing caps on bottles, putting bottles in boxes
Screwing caps on bottles, putting bottles in boxes
Screwing caps on bottles, putting bottles in boxes
When the box is full take it over to the pallet where the full boxes
    are
Tape it shut with the tape gun
And take a new box and put it where the full box was
And . . .
Screwing caps on bottles, putting bottles in boxes
Screwing caps on bottles, putting bottles in boxes
Screwing caps on bottles, putting . . .
Until Ding! Break time, Hallelujah
Take off your hairnet, peel off your gloves

Walk over to the time clock, find your card, punch out—Bing!
And everyone marches single-file up to the Common Room
And sits down with a cigarette and a coffee
Except me, I didn't drink coffee and I didn't smoke, I just sat there
And nobody saying a Word

Until Ding! Break's over
March back down, punch back in
Put on that hairnet, strap on those gloves
And start all over again and again and again and again
And day after day after day after day swirling into a giant blob of
     absolute meaninglessness (blub blub blub blub blub!)

Until this one time, my Task of the Day
Was to sit at a pumping station
Looked just like a sewing machine
Attached to a piston
Sitting in a barrel
The barrel was full of cheap suntan lotion
Two strokes from my foot pedal would activate the pump
Suck the lotion up through the hoses
Into the machine
And out the nozzle where I would be holding a bottle
Pass it to the guy on capping, and new bottle, two strokes pass
And new bottle, two strokes, pass
And new bottle, two strokes, pass
And the actual speed of the strokes was more like this

(demonstrates—there's about two or three seconds between two strokes)

And eventually
The repetition
Of the action
So totally hypnotized me
That I ceased to be able to count to two

Time and again I'd find myself holding a bottle over the nozzle
Completely unable to remember if I'd just pumped in one stroke,
Or two
Or none

So I'd hand over what would either be a normal bottle
Or a light one
Or I'd pump in a third stroke—Aaahh!
And splooge all over the place like some mad mechanical ejacula-
tion on my hand

Children's theatre

Was nothing like that

This was a good job, and I just had to remind myself of that every
now and then

And now, finally, after seven months in that fuckin' van it was time
for a little Air Travel

So we drove to the Airport

And we checked in our Stuff

And they gave us our Boarding Passes

And we gave them to the Guy

And the Guy said Thank You

Even though he wasn't Thankful

And we walked down the jetway, got on the plane, sat down,
    buckled up and took off

You know, I love air travel

The novelty on that one has not worn off in the least

I'm a little kid on Christmas morning every time I fly

And I can count on my fingers the number of times I've been on a
    plane

And they brought around snacks—I thought it was going to be
    peanuts—it wasn't—it was pretzels—and because it's a
    Canadian flight they have to print the French word for pretzels
    on the bag and the French word for pretzels is: Bretzels

Bretzels! B and a P—similar initial letter to look at and to pro-
    nounce

A clever designer could've come up with a logo where that first let-
    ter could be a B or a P depending on what you, the perceiver,
    wanted it to be

And they showed us a movie, and it was Lousy

It was Frances McDormand as a nanny in the Spanish Civil War

Some shitty straight-to-video release

I didn't watch it—I didn't have to—I didn't care—I'm flying!

I'm soaring through the air in this huge heavy machine

Something that was Absolutely Inconceivable to human beings a
mere one hundred years ago, but now we can do it with such
Accuracy and Finesse that we can land wherever we want!

And that's exactly what we did, safe and sound, in St. John's

Wasn't quite that fast

We had an overnight stop in Montreal

I happen to have a friend there, I crashed at her place

And it was cold—it's early March—the wind and the snow were
blowing against your face

But in St. John's, the next day, coldest province in the country,
supposedly

Sunny and Warm

Pleasant surprise

No trace of snow anywhere

Birds a-chirping

Sun a-shining

My relatives were waiting for me at the airport, a big gaggle of
them

Hadn't seen some of them in years

Hadn't seen others ever

And they all stood around and told me how much I'd grown

That's what relatives do

That's their job

And we all went back to my grandparents' place

And sat around the living room socializing for an hour or two

But I was tired

I don't know what it is about flying, but it really wears you down

I mean all you're doing is sitting in a chair

But it wipes you out!

Furthermore it'd been my Montreal friend's birthday the very night
before

So a bunch of us had gone out

And the bars of Montreal stay open rather late

And all

So politely, after an hour or two, I excused myself and went to the
guest room

And lay down on the guest bed

And that night I dreamed

That I was a rollerblader

So adept and agile

That I would cruise the streets and parks just looking for people
walking

Just looking for people walking normally

And when I'd spot one—I'd shoot through their legs

I was that good

I could time it just right and tuck up so tight that I could fire right
through the space of a normal person's step

Scare the hell out of 'em

In real life

I can't rollerblade

At all

(Actor goes to the person he'd given the banana to)

You finished with the banana?

(They give it back in the bag)

Thanks

(Looks inside the bag, then puts it back on the chair, repositions his feet on either side of the X)

So, the next morning I woke up, went to the St. John's Arts and
     Culture Centre and we did our show
Treasure Island, by the way—that was our show
I played Long John Silver
Maybe a bit young for the part, I do admit
But that's okay, because to an audience of nothing but kids
Anyone over eighteen is that magical thing: a Grown-Up
Someone who can drink, and smoke, and shave—all three at the
     same time if they really wanted to
Someone who pays for things outta their own wallet, and knows
     where you're supposed to go in an airport, and can
Have
Sex

Maybe I should've grown a beard, might've made me look older, or
     at least more like a pirate, but I can't
Unlike my bearded father, and his two bearded brothers, and their

bearded father—my bearded grandfather, with me something
went wrong
And the moustache part never quite connects to the beard part
And what does come in is all scraggly and thin and patchy
It's this Amish Bob Dylan look, it's just awful
So instead I wore a pirate hat and had a fake parrot on my shoulder, had a long coat and a crutch and tucked up one foot in a
loop that came out of my belt and said "Arrrrr!" a lot and it
went really well, the kids really seemed to like it
And after the show we bowed, and then packed up our stuff into
the new van, the rental van to take us to the airport to get on
the plane, the new plane, the small plane that would take us
to . . .

Labrador

So what's it like in Labrador?—I'd asked my relatives the night
before, before going to the guest room and having the
dream—what's it like
They didn't know. They'd never been.
Apart from my grandfather, who left before he was even one, didn't
remember it
Really?
"Nah. S'too expensive"
It turns out it costs more—a lot more—to fly from St. John's to
anywhere in Labrador than it does to fly from St. John's to
Toronto, or Vancouver, or Florida, or Barbados. So no one
goes.

Really?

"hyep"

That sound, I was to discover, is the Newfoundland word for yes:
  "hyep"

My Dad had always done that, and I'd never thought of it as a
  Newfoundland thing, but it is—it's this inverted "hyep," said
  while drawing in breath: "Hyep"

Can we all try that on the count of three, for no reason at all?

One, two, three

(The audience joins in:)

Hyep

Very good—it's either that or "Yis Bye"

So . . . who goes there then

"Well, no tourists, thas for sure. Mostly business people, people
  connected wid de mines"

Mines? They have mines there?

"hyep. Iron mines. Iron ore. What's left of 'em. Most of 'em closed
  down years ago"

Well then what do the people who still live there do

"Not much"

Then they showed me a book: *Coasts of Canada* by Pierre Berton

Looked like a Christmas gift—from our family

It was mostly photos, some essays of . . . the coasts of Canada: BC,
  the Arctic, Maritimes, Great Lakes, everywhere

And for Labrador there was one picture
One picture of where the wind comes off the cold, grey, icy
    Labrador Sea
And the trees along the shore had grown old, and thick, and strong
like *this!*

(A sharp horizontal motion of the hand)

Bent sharply away from that wind
Like Buster Keaton
In reverse

So, we went to the airport and we got on the new plane, the small
    plane, it was a Dash-8
I love the sound of that: a Dash-8
It's so technical, and yet so meaningless, it's like something out of
    Star Wars:
"Unleash the Dash-8s!"
Actually, to look at the thing, it looked a lot more like the plane in
    Raiders of the Lost Ark, that Indy gets on to go to Tibet—and
    there's that German agent on board, hiding behind the Life
    magazine—bald guy, big lips, burns his hand, head melts at the
    end, you know, that guy
Whatever happened to him?
That's 1981—the movie's huge—and then you never see him in
    anything, ever again
He probably lives in some house, somewhere . . .

So, like in the movie, the wings had propellers

And a guy had to come out and start them by hand

And one . . . and two . . . and three tries before it gets going . . .

And then it's going so fast you can't see it anymore, it's a perfect
circle, it's a circular blur—but within the blur you can see the
propeller and it's the size and shape of the propeller only it's
see-through and it's going really slowly, and then it slows right
down, holds still, and then it starts going the other way! How
does it do that??

And we take off

Now my relatives had not been exaggerating, there was very little
call to go to Labrador

Aside from our group—which was four of us—including me

There was one other passenger—this pop-eyed bearded fat guy, sitting there, white-knuckling his armrests

They brought around snacks—more bretzels

I ate 'em, and read my book

Timequake, by Kurt Vonnegut—that's what I was reading

Great book, excellent book

And perfect airplane reading, because Vonnegut always writes in
these short little bursts, separated by a line, or an asterisk,
or an R

So it's very easy when you're flying to just read a little bit, and then
look out the window, and then read a little bit, and then pay
attention to the Safety Lecture, and then read a little bit, and
then order a drink

And it's not only easy to come back, but you're always glad you
did, because Vonnegut's so original, and funny, and awesome

There's so many good books out there—not just by him but by a
    lot of people

And this is tremendously exciting to me because I am a Bibliophile

Which is weird because I was a mediocre English student in high
    school and university until I found the writers I liked—the
    ones that spoke right to me

Charles Bukowski! John Fante!

Words like green and yellow and blue flames

JP Donleavy! Stephen Leacock!

Images, sentences just knocking me out of my chair!

Aldous Huxley! Sinclair Lewis!

Whoa! What a feeling!

Raymond Carver! Sherwood Anderson!

How come no one told me about this before? Why was this magic
    kept a secret?

You know what the best part is? The best, craziest part of all:

None of them ever write about anything!

There's no plot! Or very little, anyway—there's no suspense—king-
    doms are never falling—it's just this befuddled main character
    trying to make his way in the world

Some guy, sitting in a chair

Noticing for the first time in his life

The way the light bounces in between the ice cubes in his glass

And then mashing out a cigarette

And looking out the window

Not even knowing what to think

And for some reason
Every detail
Is fascinating

And luminous

And infinite

So that's what I did on the plane, dipped into my little world of
    magic
And like it's very easy to do with Vonnegut I'd read a little bit, and
    then look out the window
Trees
And then read a little bit, and then look out the window
Rock—Newfoundland is nicknamed "The Rock" for a very good
    reason—large portions of it look like the moon
And then read a little bit, and then look out the window
Water—there it is—the cold, grey, icy Labrador Sea—would not
    want to crash into that
And then: clouds. Clouds like I've never seen 'em before—this big
    white bank of cotton candy clouds, the size of a mountain
    range
And . . . Thoonk!
We fly right into 'em

Visibility: Zero

It's as if we've just flown into a blank sheet of paper

A landscape God forgot to draw

Our destination, by the way, was Wabush
Wabush, Labrador, where the airport is, fifteen minutes from where
    we'd be performing:
Labrador City
Labrador City! Where my grandfather's from—fantastic coinci-
    dence there
But furthermore it sounded so good—so big! I mean, it's named
    after the whole damn place—and it's a city! With a whole sepa-
    rate word and a capital C
I like cities—they're big and exciting and things happen in them

But furthermore there was something else, something intangible
It's as if there was something there
Something waiting
Something coming

(The actor then steps out of the light and rearranges the items on stage with slow, careful deliberation.

The chair is brought a bit closer to the X.

A single cushion is placed about a foot and a half behind the X.

The remaining five cushions are piled into a crash pad in the darkness, stage right of the spotlight.

The banana peel is removed from the brown bag and placed in front of the crash pad.

The paper bag is put to the side, out of the way.

The actor checks that everything is where it should be, and makes minor adjustments if necessary before returning to the spotlight and carefully placing his feet on either side of the X, yet again.)

So we began our descent

Whoom!

You know that feeling, it's like the plane just dropped two hundred
    metres but your stomach stayed up there

Whoom!

And the wind is bucking us from side to side to side like a giant
    playing with a soccer ball

And outside my window it's still the same blank sheet of paper, I
    don't know how or where we're going to land but we are
    because the wheels are down on the wings

And Whoom! Whoom!

And suddenly the ground just Appears—Pavement—a wind-swept
    runway

But the wind's bucking us worse than ever

We are a ball in the bingo machine
And we
Touch
Down

Soffffft

Like a ballerina sneaking across the carpet

And then taxi in and up to the dinkiest little airport I have ever seen
Looked like an army bunker, buried in the snow
And we stopped
And we stayed there
And there's no jetway
A grounds attendant, bundled up like an astronaut, wheels a stair-
    case up to the door
You're gonna have to walk
They announced the temperature outside
Seventy-four degrees
below zero
plus a wind chill factor of up to fifty kilometres per hour
and it's snowing

Get ready, Vancouver boy.
I was, I hoped:
Long johns, toque, boots, mitts, parka, scarf
Most of it borrowed from my uncle Randy
By an astounding coincidence Uncle Randy and I have the same
    sized feet

So they lined us up at the door, I was first, they opened the door
and . . .

Holy fuck

HOLY FUCK IT'S COLD

The wind

That wind! Slicing through that parka like a Cutco knife
But my legs knew what to do: *Run!!!*
Never, in all my years of high-school track, had I run that fast
And up against the door and . . . inside

Oh Fuck . . . holy Christ . . . oh my fucking Christ
And there's this guy, this guy standing above me, just beaming with
    delight

"Nat bad, ehn?"
What?
"The cold—nat bad, innit?"
Yeah
"I'm Sean"
Hi Sean
"I'm from the Arts and Culture"
Oh! Hi
I stood up, introduced myself and then we kind of stood there,
    staring at each other

(pause)

It's really fucking cold here Sean

"Ah, that's nuttin'. On Sunday it was down to 99 below. Hyep.
    Plus de wind chill. One time, out at de mines, it got down to
    150 below. Hyep. 150 below . . . actually, it got colder than
    dat, but no one knows by how much, cuz in the marnin' dey
    found the gauges all cracked in half, frozen solid, saying '150
    below! 150 below!' ah-Hah-Hah-Hah-Hah!!!"

We piled our stuff into the back of Sean's jeep—truck—I'm not
    quite sure what you call those things—it was one of those
    Operation Desert Storm-Mobiles

I don't know how he knew where he was going in this whiteout

But Sean drove at full speed, with complete confidence, and looked
    over at you as he told you a funny story

But, before you knew it, we pulled up safe and sound to our motel:
    The Two Seasons Inn

That's the name?? The name on the sign? The Two Seasons Inn??

"Hyep. Two seasons, bye. Winter . . . and winter! Ah-Hah-Hah-
    Hah-Hah!!"

We dashed inside and checked in at the desk and settled into our
    rooms, our individual motel rooms, standardized, homoge-
    nized, and sanitized for your protection

Okay, familiar territory at last

I mean, I've been touring children's theatre for seven months at this
    point, I've been in a hundred motel rooms, they are identical—
    a motel's a motel's a motel's a motel, as Gertrude Stein once said

But this motel room
Is in Labrador

So I walked over to the sink
Turned on the tap

That's Labrador water
The colour of weak tea, incidentally

The phone book
The phone book said "Labrador"
Every single person in that book lives in Labrador

I went to the window, drew back the curtains
There was a view
You could see blowing snow
And a couple of distant buildings that looked like army bunkers,
    buried in the snow

Well, this is it
Here we are
Welcome to Labrador, boy
Welcome Home

Fucking Greenland!
Why—Why—WHY would any ancestor of mine come HERE
And STAY???
And allow their children to stay
Would you live here—is working in an iron mine that much fun?

The tourist brochure on the nightstand said:
"Visit Labrador, it's the Land of Cain"

That's their tourist slogan? The Land of Cain??
"And Cain so cruelly killed his brother Abel that the Lord God
    spake unto him, saying 'Cain. Given that thy sin is so vile and
    heinous, thou shalt live in a land equally vile and heinous. I
    banish thee to live in Labrador!!'"

Holy shit

That's a mirror

I thought it was my Dad

I was still wearing Uncle Randy's parka, and the hood was up, and
    Goddam if I didn't look exactly like the first ever photos taken
    of my Dad, in the Yukon, in the seventies

Well that caps off a great day
Great year. It'd been a helluva year for things like that
They found my first grey hair at a haircut in October
I got glasses for the first time in my life in November
My tall, skinny guy, insatiable appetite had finally died down
I was turning into my Dad by degrees
Hadn't checked my progress in a while
And now it seems
The only thing keeping us apart
Was

A Parka

All right then

It is now time

To get

DRUNK

Hell yeah, dour realization hits you like that, there is one solution:
     the Bottle

Actually, I'm not much of a drinker
I don't mind a good pint now and then
But too much of the stuff makes me melancholy and stupid and
     ugly
Give me a nice fat joint any day of the week
And I am happy and creative and sensual and brilliant
And reeling off the words and the stories and the opinions at a mil-
     lion miles a second
And they all come together and they all make sense which is how I
     got doing one-person shows in the first place
Used to do 'em inadvertently

But in Labrador
Where ya gonna find any

So the bottle it'll have to be

So I walked to the front desk and asked the woman there if she
    could recommend a good place for a guy to get hammered
She could—she could even point to it—you could see it out the
    window
It was this kind of an army bunker, buried in the snow
Is that a good place to drink?
"Hyep. The whole town goes dere"

Town. It was a town. It was the township of Labrador CITY
How'd they figure that one?
Did they just choose the word "City" because it sounded nice?
It's like how there's this town/city in Japan that about ten years ago
    officially changed its name to "Usa"—Usa, Japan—so that they
    could manufacture things and then stamp on those things
    "Made in Usa"—U-S-A
True story
My Dad told me that

All right, strap up, wrap up, bundle up tight
Up against that door and . . . out that door you go
Holy Fuck it's cold! Run, boy Run Run Run!

NO

Don't Run

It's solid ice
How did this happen?
I don't know

But if you go any faster than two inches at a time you're going to
     do one of those spectacular Charlie Chaplin ZOOP! falls where
     your legs fly out from under you and you hang in the air for a
     second and then HONK! land on your tailbone on the ice
No Thank You
So I'm walking two inches at a time
Old man steps, baby steps
And the wind—the wind is slicing across my face like a whip
     wielded by Satan himself
Ahhh
What kind of a bizarre hell is this where it's too cold to be outside
     for even five seconds, and yet it's too icy to walk any faster
     than a goddam turtle!
What am I doing here? Get me out of here!
Put me in an environment I understand
Give me a living room with hardwood floors and high ceilings and
     plants and good videos and CDs and books on the shelves and
     someone playing something on acoustic guitar and someone
     cooking something that involves chickpeas get me out of
     here!!!

And . . . inside
Holy fuck—oh my fucking God—holy fucking Christ

(pause)

Get a load of this place

It's *The Lord of the Rings*

These thick wooden chairs and thick wooden tables
Like they grew there
And a blazing firepit—oh, God—warmth has never felt soooo
    goood . . .
And music—there's a band—a three-piece band squashed in the
    corner
One guy on fiddle, one guy on the little button accordion, and one
    guy on the drum—that Irish hand-drum—jugga-da jugga-da
    jugga-da jugga-da . . .

And the people—they're packed in so tight and dancing so hard
    that there's sparks
There's little green sparks where their bootnails hit the floornails

And look at these people
These men—these bearded, chesty, Lord of the Rings tree-stump
    men
And the women

The Women . . .

You know, there is something about the difficult places
Ireland
Poland
Russia
Labrador
The hard earth just brings out the most beautiful women

Like flowers in the snow

But they are all staked, claimed and spoken for, you can count on that
Because I'm already getting dirty looks from some of those tree
    stumps
And I'm not here for that
I am not here for that
I am here to get pleasantly, and privately obliterated

So, I avert my eyes and work my way through the crowd up to the
    bar, or, as they call it in Lab City, the "Bair"
And the Bairtender takes one look at me and says
"You're not from around here, arya bye"
No
"Whereya from den"
Vancouver
"Vancouver?? Whaddaya doin' 'ere?"
Children's theatre
"Well, you're a lang ways from home, bye"
Yeah

Okay—now people are starting to look
It's not like the band stopped when I came in, dramatic though my
    entrance was
It's loud and it's crowded
But the people nearby are looking
Cuz I'm obviously new and they just don't get new people here that
    often

"Y'ever been screeched in, bye?"
What?

"Screeched—y'ever been screeched?"

Nope

Oh, shit

I should've said yes

I don't quite know what he means, but I should've said yes

I've heard of screech—vaguely—like you hear about a sasquatch

It's this Newfoundland moonshine

It's either grain alcohol or cod alcohol

That gets pumped into an empty rum barrel

And it's left to sit there for two or three months to absorb the bilge,
     the scrapings

It's the afterbirth of rum, basically

And as I mentioned I'm no drinker

And Boom Boom Boom Boom

These four big shot glasses appear on the bar in front of me

And RINGDINGDINGDING-DINGDINGDINGDING-
     DINGDINGDINGDING-DING!

The bartender's ringing the bell

And the band stops

The conversations stop

The heads turn

And the bartender says

"Ladies and Gentlemen—we gats a special treat for you, 'ere at de
     bair tonight—we have wit' us a young man, from Vancouver,
     British Columbia, who's never been screeched"

"HO-AY!!!!!"

BOOM BOOM BOOM BOOM BOOM

They're banging their big meaty tree-root fists on their tables in
    rhythm
And the bairtender takes this unmairked jair from under de bair
And twists off the lid
And fills those four shot glasses with this murky off-white off-
    brown Stuff that's halfway in between being maple syrup and
    halfway in between being something I once saw in a nightmare
    when I was sixteen years old
And he replaces the lid and says
"Now 'eres how it works, bye. We're gonna say 'Is you or Is you nat
    a Screecher' and you're gonna say 'Indeed I is, me auld Cock,
    and Lang may your Big Jib Draw'"
Long what???
"Lang may your Big Jib Draw"
Your big jib . . .
"Ah—no practicin' dere, bye. And den you takes all four-a dese
    shats, ya drinks 'em all at de same time"
And he puts his hands over mine into a kind of diamond shape
    and pushes the glasses together and click . . . click . . . click
    click!
They fit together
How did they do that
I don't know
But I don't like it
Now I can only lift them and drink them as one

Now, here's the part of the show where I need you, the audience, to
    be the people in the bar that night
Now as if you're an audience of chesty, tree-stump men and it's

seventy-four below outside, plus wind-chill, I need you to say,
   on your cue line—which is "Fuck Fuck Fuck":
"Is you, or Is you Nat, a Screecher"
Let's try that once to practice
Fuck Fuck Fuck

(The audience says "Is you, or Is you Nat, a Screecher")

Good! Now remember your cue, it's the third Fuck

Now, everybody's looking at me with these big, evil leers
They know exactly what I've got coming
And I told ya, I'm no drinker
I suffered through all those bullshit teenage rites of passage and
   took it like it was medicine, but ah Fuck Fuck Fuck

(Audience: "Is you, or Is you Nat, a Screecher")

Okay—pretty good, but we're working towards a climax—let's try
   one more time, with feeling

And everybody's looking at me with those big evil leers
They know exactly what I've got coming
And I told ya, I ain't no drinker
I suffered through all those bullshit teenage rites of passage and
   took it like it was medicine, but ah Fuck . . . Fuck . . . FUCK!

(Audience: "Is You, or Is You Nat, a Screecher!!")

Indeed I Is, me Old Cock . . .

And Long May Your Big . . . Jib . . . Draw

(Knocks back the four shots at once

Reels

Almost retches

Recovers

Shakes it off)

Not bad . . .

"HO-AYY!!!"

And the band starts back up and everyone's clapping me on the
    back way too hard
Okay—Okay
And Boom! This tankard of foaming beer appears on the bar in
    front of me
And the Bartender says
"'at one's on de house, bye—you're de straight goods, you is"
Well, you know why—it's cuz my grandfather's from here
"From Lab City?"
hyep
"Well—what's 'is name den"

So I told him
Not a glimmer of recognition
No? That's not a common last name here?
"Nah. I never heard of it"
Oh. Well, so much for that, then
Guess I should-a figured
With all the men looking like tree stumps
Instead-a bean poles

Ahh—the mirrors in this place

(Does a big shiver—the Hard Liquor Shiver—then recovers)

That's the thing I hate most about Hard Liquor is the aftershocks
The aftershocks
They wait thirty seconds, or a minute, and then make me do Jerry
    Lewis takes:
"Nyaahh!!"

That's no mirror

That's my Dad

That's my Dad without a beard

What the hell? Who is this guy?

But he's looking at me with the same confused face I've got
And he works his way through the crowd

And comes right up to me and says
"You looks just like my son Mike"
You look just like my Dad
"Where is 'e den"
Vancouver. Where's Mike?
"'E's dead"
Oh
"Died in de mines"
Oh

So I told him my grandfather's name—he knew it!
It was his uncle—who'd left as a baby with my great-grandfather—
    and they'd changed their names and never heard from them
    again

So—we're related—you're—what—my second . . . uncle?
"hyep"

And looking at the guy he wasn't clean-shaven—not quite
He did have a beard
But it didn't connect to the moustache
And the rest came in all scraggly and thin
and patchy

Tell me about Mike—what was he like
"Ah—'E was the best lad in the world, dat bye was. 'E could get de
    whole room goin', tellin' his stories"
Really?
"hyep. Big ol' crowded bair like dis one—everyone'd be standing

around Mike, Mike'd be talking up a storm, making everyone
    laugh"
Really
"Yis bye. And 'e was married"
Really!
"hyep. Dat's his wife over dere—well, widow—she wit' some other
    feller now . . ."

So I looked

There she was

The most

The most beautiful woman

In the world

I mean, I know guys say that fifteen times a week

But

She was The One

So I excused myself and worked my way through the crowd

And as I got about halfway there she could see some guy coming
   towards her

So she looked up

All confused

And scared

But then not

It was okay

So I kept coming

And as I got closer I could see she's sitting by herself

Only empty chair

In the whole place

(Places the chair in the middle of the spotlight)

So I sat down

(Sits down on the chair)

And I didn't say anything
And she didn't say anything
What do you say?

And then taptaptap on my shoulder
Yeah?
And Wham!

(Falls backward off the chair onto the floor)

Knocked off my chair by the biggest fattest ugliest tree stump of
    them all
And he's yelling at her and he's yelling at me in this thick
    Newfoundland gibberish
And I don't quite know what he's saying but I get the idea
As I'm backing away and he comes up and kicks me—Ow
And kicks me—Okay, Okay!
And up against the wall and along the wall
And up against the door and out the door
HOLY FUCK IT'S COLD
Run Boy, Run Run Run!
On the ice, that is a very big mistake

(Slips on the banana peel, onto the crashpad of cushions)

Ohhhh

Ohhh fuck that hurt
Holy fuck it's cold
He's got a shovel
What the fuck does a guy like that need a shovel for

I'm gonna die

Holy shit I'm gonna die! Here! Like this!

I just hope someone tells the truth at my funeral

And WHAM

mmmmm . . .

(Goes limp. He's scrambled into the dark part of the stage, by the way)

(Pause)

And . . . Blackout
The blackout represents me blacking out

Pause in the darkness

Pause represents unconsciousness

(The actor's gathering up the banana peel into the bag, up-ending the chair and putting the cushions into their original pile throughout this bit)

And then Lights Up
Lights Up represents me waking up
Rescued by my sort-of father and sort-of wife

And I'm bruised
And I'm fat-lipped
And I'm sore
But I'm okay, you know

Not Dead

And then Healing
And how good that feels

To go through all that pain
And then make it across to the other side

In some odd way it makes the whole thing worth having gone
    through in the first place
Makes you realize how good it feels just to be healthy
Just to be normal
Just to be alive

And then . . . lights down

End it there

Nice note of hope like that

End it there
Lights up, with music
Curtain call
Applause, bowing
Lights down again
Lights up, with house lights
Everyone gets up and leaves

And that

Would be that

(Resuming his spot on the X)

Except for the fact that I've been lying to you all for a good long
    time now

Labrador was cold, but it wasn't that bad
The mines are alive and well
The average income in Lab City is eighty thousand a year
Everyone has a nice house and a new skidoo
Sean, the guy that picked us up at the airport, didn't talk like that,
    didn't make those jokes
The motel was a hotel—it was called the Two Seasons Inn—and it
    was nice—nicest place we stayed all tour
And the bar was just a bar
Neon signs, commercial beer on tap, guy with an electric guitar
    and a drum machine playing "Hotel California"

And no one batted an eye when I walked in
I sat down at one of the many empty tables
Had my pint, read my book, and left
And that was Labrador

I did get screeched in, but in St. John's
Which only involved drinking one shot of screech
Which is good rum, it's made in Jamaica

And my grandfather's not even from Labrador
He is from St. John's—he lives there still
And he doesn't have a beard—minor detail, I know
My Dad has a beard—had a beard—he shaved it
And I'm like my Dad in some ways
I'm not like him in other ways
And I didn't get drunk when I realized that

You know

If a race of aliens

From outer space

Were to study us

From our one-person shows

And nothing else

They'd come up with the conclusion that every single human being
    on this planet had a life that was *Unbelievably Exciting!!*
This roller-coaster ride of thrills and spills and chills
Leading up to this climax, this flash of truth, this Revelation
That made everything so much easier for that person from that
    point on

And that's fine, I guess

But for me, revelations are few and far between
And most of my days slide off the windowsill
Into oblivion

And that's okay too

I'm no hero
I'm just a guy
I'm up and down

I get depressed sometimes for no reason

I remember the oddest things

And I'm never really that sure
Of what's

Going on

Lights down,

Fade

To Black

(Lights down, fade to black.

Lights and music up for curtain call.)

THE END

About the Author

TJ Dawe is a Vancouver-based writer and performer who has toured extensively throughout North America and Australia. In 1998, his play *Tired Clichés* received a Jessie Richardson Award for Best New Play or Musical. In 2001, *The Slip-Knot* received the Just For Laughs Comedy Award in Montreal, was remounted at the Just For Laughs On the Edge series, and won the Best Male Performer award at the 2002 Orlando International Fringe Festival.

His shows, which combine elements of stand-up comedy, music, and physical theatre to explore serious subjects, have drawn comparisons to Lord Buckley, Jerry Seinfeld and Eric Bogosian.

Plays by TJ Dawe

Whank, 1997
Stating the Obvious, 1997
Tired Clichés, 1998
Labrador, 1999
Constable Sparky and the Mystery Pirate Orphan, or *Fort Steele in Flames: a Rolicking Comedy, with Songs*, co-written with Michael Rinaldi, 2000
52 Pick-up, co-written with Rita Bozi, 2000
The Slip-Knot, 2001
The Doctor is Sick, adapted from Anthony Burgess, 2002
Constable Sparky and the Curse of the Hoodwinked Swede, co-written with Michael Rinaldi, 2002
Tracks, adapted from Jack London, 2002
Toothpaste & Cigars, co-written with Michael Rinaldi, 2003
The Power of Ignorance, co-written with Chris Gibbs, 2003
A Canadian Bartender at Butlin's, 2003

By turns hysterical and heartbreaking, frantic and thoughtful, The Slip-Knot is a spellbinding comic monologue unlike any other. Journey with the incomparable TJ Dawe as he mans a giant truck, becomes the unhelpful voice on the other end of the phone line, and takes stock of euphemisms while he stocks the shelves in a drugstore. In between are ruminations and wise observations on long-distance relationships, the history of Santa Claus, recreational Gravol, and why you should never mail meat, no matter what the clerk at the 7-11 tells you.

WINNER, JUST FOR LAUGHS COMEDY AWARD

Hilarious and surreal . . . a scintillating
explosion of imagination.
—*Hour* (Montreal)

TJ Dawe is unnervingly captivating, increasingly edgy,
and brilliantly funny.
—*Adelaide Advertiser* (Australia)

If you could listen to a juggler, and if that juggler were the
most accomplished juggler in the world, the experience would
be something like listening to TJ Dawe in *The Slip-Knot.*
—*Orlando Sentinel* (Florida)